MY
VILLAGE
QUEENS

By

Dr. Clarice Ford-Kulah

Artist

Wilma Stryker Roberts

DEDICATED TO MY BEAUTIFUL AFRICAN WARRIOR CHILDREN

Jordan, Bart, Wrenii, and Wrenelle

ISBN: 9781667868141

Printed in the United States of America

My name is Mardea Johnson! My name means "new woman" in Bassa.
I was born in a small Bassa village in Liberia, West Africa.

I was raised by five beautiful, hardworking women. One was my mother, SuaKoko and the others were her four sisters, my remarkable aunties, Yaa Asantewaa, Amina, Nzinga, and Dahomey.

 I know all their names do not sound like traditional Liberian names, but that is because my grandma was a progressive woman who believed in all of Africa being represented. She wanted each of her daughters named after strong warrior women that represented Africa well.

Let's start with SuaKoko. She fought many battles to protect her land. She later became paramount chief of her town in modern-day Liberia and served as supplier for the Harvard Medical African Expedition.

Yaa Asantewaa was the Queen Mother of Ejisu in the Ashanti Empire in modern-day Ghana. She led the Ashanti War against the British Empire.

Queen Amina was a ruthless warrior of Nigeria who led an army of about 20,000 men.

Nzinga was queen of the Mbundu people of modern-day Angola. She fought against the Portuguese to protect her people from the expanding slave trade.

The Dahomey Amazons were an all-female militia group of modern-day Benin that fought against slavery when most of the men were enslaved.

In our village, the ladies did the cooking and cleaning. My mother, Suakoko, on the left, did most of the shopping in the market. Her sister, Yaa Asantewaa, did most of the cleaning, but also helped my mom with the cooking.

While they cooked together, they sang traditional songs, laughed, and enjoyed conversation about family, history, and so much more.

The other three sisters, Amina, Nzinga, and Dahomey were responsible for fetching water from the creek, washing the clothes, and sometimes purchasing additional groceries from the market that my mom may have forgotten. On their way to and from the market, my aunt Amina always carried her baby on her back and the drawing bucket in her hand.

My other two aunts Nzinga and Dahomey also carried buckets and items from the market, sometimes on their heads. As they walked, they told amazing stories and shared ideas about how to make our village better.

Aunty Amina, just like my mom and all my aunties, after working all day and caring for their children, would put her baby to sleep and beat fufu in the mortar. The mortar works just like the blender. Instead of pressing a button to blend, we beat the ingredients in the mortar.

Now, besides my four amazing aunties, there were other women that made a difference in my life. These women were also known as my aunties. You see, in African villages, all the older women are called aunties and the older men are called uncles.

That means you must always be good and respectful because any of them can chastise you for doing the wrong things. And if they spank you, there is nothing you can do about it. If you try to tell your mommy, she will only side with them. Sometimes, she may even give you another spanking. I know it sounds different, but that is our culture.

And to be honest, I love this culture. It has helped to mold me into the respectful and honest young lady that I am. It has given me a chance to learn from my mom and aunties. Watching them getting up early in the morning, fetching water from the stream, going to the market, washing clothes by the riverside, cooking, and cleaning, even when they were tired, has made me to understand and embrace my own strength.

I know it was hard work, but these women persevered and raised wonderful families and strong daughters like me. I learned so much from them, like how to be an intelligent, skillful woman and still take care of a husband, children, and the entire family.

Today, I stand as Mardea, queen of my mother's town, a village filled with powerful women, wives, and brilliant queens.

AUTHOR'S NOTE

Since the dawn of time, African women have been the backbones of their families. Many have not only worked in the home, but outside the home. During slavery, when many of the men were taken away from their villages, the women stepped in and served as warriors to protect their families. To date, no children's books or movies have been written about them. Women like Madame SuaKoko of Liberia, Yaa Asantewaa of Ghana, Queen Amina of Nigeria, Queen Nzinga of Angola, the Dahomey Amazons of Benin.

As we embrace our past and look forward to a brighter future for African women, let us be inclusive in our stories. Let's provide young African girls strong women figure and role models that they can look up to, women like Ellen Johnson Sirleaf- first female president elected in Africa, Amina Mohammad-Deputy Secretary General of the United Nations, Lucy Quist-CEO of Airtel Ghana, Dr. Martha Namundjebo-Talabun- Chairperson of the United Africa Group, just to name a few.

It is my hope and prayer that this book pays homage to all the wonderful women warriors that went before us!

If you would like to purchase any of the dolls pictured in this book, please call 770 755 2400!

Thanks and God Bless You!